CW01582435

IN THE EVANGELICAL WAY

Children, Young People and the Church
in Evangelical Parishes of the Church of England

A companion to *Continuing in the Way*

LESLIE J FRANCIS AND DAVID W LANKSHEAR

THE NATIONAL SOCIETY (CHURCH OF ENGLAND)
FOR PROMOTING RELIGIOUS EDUCATION

ISBN 0 901819 38 7

Published 1995 by the National Society

Copyright © Leslie J Francis and David W Lankshear, 1995. This publication may not be reproduced, either in whole or in part, whether for sale or otherwise, without written permission which should be sought from The National Society, Church House, Great Smith Street, London SW1P 3NZ.

Printed in England by Bourne Press Ltd

Preface

Just before the start of the Decade of Evangelism the Church's work with the young was reassessed in a profoundly influential report: *Children in the Way* (National Society/Church House Publishing, 1988). As the Decade continues other publications have marked developments in this vitally important area of the Church's mission: among them are *All God's Children* (NS/CHP, 1991) and *Continuing in the Way* (NS, 1991), in which Leslie Francis and David Lankshear built up a comprehensive picture of the Church of England's involvement in the lives of children and young people up to the age of twenty-one. Further research and analysis has led to the production of *In the Evangelical Way*, a study of the contact which Anglican churches of the Evangelical tradition have with the young. The National Society has also published a companion volume, *In the Catholic Way*.

The Authors

The authors have collaborated on many pieces of research into young people, education and the churches. They are the Editors of *Christian Perspectives on Church Schools: a reader* (Gracewing, 1993).

David W Lankshear is Deputy Secretary of the National Society and Schools Officer of the General Synod Board of Education. His previous publications include *Looking for Quality in a Church School* (NS, 1992), *A Shared Vision* (NS, 1992), *Preparing for Inspection in a Church School* (NS, 1993) and, with Alan Brown, *Inspection Handbook for Church Schools* (NS, 1995).

Leslie J Francis is D J James Professor of Pastoral Theology at Trinity College, Carmarthen, and the University of Wales, Lampeter. His previous publications include *Partnership in Rural Education* (Collins, 1986), *Christian Perspectives on Education* (Gracewing, 1989) and *Christian Perspectives on Faith Development* (Gracewing, 1992).

The authors' address for correspondence is Trinity College, Carmarthen, Dyfed SA31 3EP

Introduction

A decade after the British Council of Churches' influential report *The Child in the Church*[1] the National Conference of Religious Education and Children's Work Advisers set up a working party to examine the place of children and young people in the Church of England. The conference recognised that recommendations for future policy and action needed to be anchored in a realistic appreciation of contemporary starting points, and so with this in mind it commissioned a high-quality survey.

A detailed questionnaire was sent to every church or habitual place of worship between February 1986 and July 1987 throughout twenty-four whole dioceses and the archdeaconry of the Isle of Wight. This involved a total of 9,909 places of worship.

After a lengthy process of pursuing non-respondents 7,157 thoroughly completed questionnaires were returned, giving the satisfactory response rate of 72.2% among the participating dioceses and representing 42.8% of all the churches in the forty-three dioceses of England.

The questionnaire was developed from the one first used by Leslie Francis in his study *Rural Anglicanism*[2]. The three parts of this questionnaire examine key background information about the churches, membership and participation in a range of activities, and a detailed log of services and activities over an eight day period from Sunday to Sunday.

The initial findings from this survey, based on an interim database and focusing on the Church of England's contact with children up to the age of thirteen years, were presented in chapter seven of *Children in the Way*, published in 1988[3]. After considerably more work had been invested in the database a further picture, based on all the responding churches and including young people up to the age of twenty-one, was presented in *Continuing in the Way*, published in 1991[4].

At the same time the present authors have been engaged in a series of more sophisticated analyses of these data to address questions of fundamental importance to the Churches. Work so far completed includes an assessment of the impact of Church schools on rural[5] and urban[6] church life, the contribution of Sunday schools to the rural church[7], all-age learning and worship[8], the churches' role in pre-school provision in rural[9] and urban[10] environments, the use of the revised catechism in Anglican churches[11], the role of the rural rectory and the impact of a resident priest on local church life[12], the place of children and young people in church life within hamlets of fewer than 250 inhabitants[13], the difficulties faced by small congregations in making contact with the young[14], the relationship between ageing clergy and church life in rural and suburban parishes[15], a detailed profile of Anglicanism on the Isle of Wight[16], and an examination of the range of special services and events which provide contact between the Church of England and young people[17]. Analyses of this nature demonstrate how data collected through well-conducted surveys can be reprocessed to throw new light on key issues of practical theology.

Surveys of this calibre are expensive to undertake and time consuming to analyse. Like the nationwide secular census, this survey should provide the Church of England with a valuable resource for evaluation and planning through a period of some ten years. Further analyses of these data are therefore still under way. These data are, after all, still the most comprehensive and most up to date statistical source of information currently available. A decade after the original study, however, this survey will clearly require replication. The original survey was designed with such a possibility in mind and could act as the foundation study against which future trends may be carefully monitored and interpreted.

The Evangelical Way

The analysis presented in this booklet profiles the contribution being made by Evangelical parishes within the Church of England as a whole. In comparison with the overall picture of the Church of England's contact with children and young people presented in *Continuing in the Way*[18] this analysis interrogates the database in order to discern how the performance of Evangelical parishes measured against the overall performance of the Church of England. Are Evangelical parishes conforming to the average expectation of Church of England churches, are they performing better in some areas, or are they performing less well in some areas? Knowledge of this nature should enable the Evangelical movement to respond more effectively to the Decade of Evangelism. This analysis complements the study made of Catholic parishes in the companion volume, *In the Catholic Way*[19].

Envisaging the potential value of such questions, the survey had asked those completing the original questionnaires to assess the churchmanship of each worship centre on a seven point scale, ranging from very Evangelical through middle of the road, to very Catholic. For the purposes of the present analysis, Evangelical churches were defined as those rated one or two at the Evangelical end of the seven point continuum.

Overall, 16% of the 7,157 churches and worship centres participating in the survey were identified as Evangelical according to this criterion. Table 1 explores how the proportion of Evangelical churches or worship centres varies from diocese to diocese. This information is set in the context of the number of worship centres within each participating diocese and the proportion of these worship centres for which a questionnaire was returned.

From this table it can be seen that the response rate varied from 52% in the Diocese of Hereford to 97% in the Diocese of Worcester and 100% on the Isle of Wight. The league table of Evangelical churches reads as follows: St Albans (9%), Worcester (9%), Hereford (10%), Peterborough (10%), Oxford (11%), Ely (12%), Isle of Wight (12%), Durham (13%), Truro (13%), York (13%), Gloucester (15%), Lichfield (15%), Salisbury (15%), Birmingham (16%), Carlisle (16%), Bath and Wells (17%), Bristol

Table 1 Response rate and Evangelical churches by diocese

Diocese	Number of worship centres	Number of replies	Response %	Evangelical %
Bath and Wells	586	475	82	17
Birmingham	207	174	84	16
Blackburn	293	226	77	21
Bristol	210	184	88	17
Carlisle	340	270	79	16
Chelmsford	576	338	59	31
Chester	374	274	73	23
Chichester	512	368	72	19
Derby	345	209	61	17
Durham	309	190	61	13
Ely	328	210	64	12
Gloucester	408	345	85	15
Hereford	403	208	52	10
Isle of Wight	61	61	100	12
Lichfield	614	479	78	15
London	484	322	67	21
Oxford	824	535	65	11
Peterborough	374	262	70	10
St Albans	393	282	72	9
Salisbury	575	430	75	15
Sheffield	214	122	57	25
Southwell	300	247	82	23
Truro	301	248	82	13
Worcester	260	253	97	9
York	618	445	72	13

(17%), Derby (17%), Chichester (19%), Blackburn (21%), London (21%), Chester (23%), Southwell (23%), Sheffield (25%) and Chelmsford (31%). It is interesting to note that some of the dioceses which claim a higher than average proportion of Evangelical parishes also claim a higher than average proportion of Catholic parishes. Blackburn, Chichester and London all fall into this category. This may indicate a tendency in some dioceses towards the polarisation of self-expressed churchmanship preferences.

The data also reveal clear relationships between the proportion of Evangelical churches and both social class and the distinctions between urban and rural environment. Thus, 18% of the churches in areas where less than a third of the houses are owner-occupied identify themselves as Evangelical, compared with 15% of the churches in areas where the majority of houses are owner occupied. In urban and inner-city areas 25% of the churches identify themselves as Evangelical, compared with 13% in villages, 14% in market towns, 19% in large towns, 21% in new towns, 21% in large housing estates and 19% in suburbia.

Presenting the Findings

The findings of this comparison between the overall picture presented by Church of England churches and the picture presented by those churches identified as Evangelical are now displayed systematically in seven sections, following the model established in *Continuing in the Way*. These sections deal in turn with initiation statistics, provision for pre-schoolers, Sunday schools and Church Pastoral Aid Society provision, participation in services, uniformed groups, other youth provision and the Sunday picture.

On the assumption that the responding churches provide an accurate picture of the Church of England as a whole, the figures given by this sample are grossed up to furnish an estimate of the number of individuals in touch with the Church of England as a whole and with Evangelical churches in particular throughout the forty-three home dioceses (rounded to the nearest ten). Information is presented separately for each of the six age groups, namely the under two year olds, two to five year olds, six to nine year olds, ten to thirteen year olds, fourteen to seventeen year olds and eighteen to twenty-one year olds.

Each table presents five pieces of information in relationship to every relevant age group. The first column presents an estimate of the number of individuals involved throughout the Church of England. The second column presents an estimate of the number of individuals involved in Evangelical churches. The third column calculates the number of individuals involved in Evangelical churches as a percentage of those involved throughout the Church of England as a whole. Since 16% of all the churches are identified as Evangelical, this third column should stand at 16% if the Evangelical sector is performing according to the average expectation of Church of England churches. When this figure falls below 16% it suggests that Evangelical churches are performing less well than average. When this figure rises above 16% it suggests that Evangelical churches are performing better than average. The fourth column presents the percentage of Church of England churches as a whole which report involvement in the specified area of activity in terms of contact with at least one person within the age group. The fifth column presents the percentage of Evangelical churches reporting involvement in the same activity. Comparison between these two percentages indicates the level of involvement of Evangelical churches alongside the average expectation for Church of England churches.

From time to time throughout the text the churches' contact with specific age groups is expressed as a percentage of the total population in England of that age. This is made possible by comparison with the population estimate for 1986 published by the Office of Population Censuses and Surveys[20].

Initiation Rites

Baptism

The baptism figures collected by the survey were for the year 1985. Table two makes it clear that Evangelical churches are less actively involved in the baptism of infants and children than is the case throughout the Church of England as a whole. The 16% of churches identified as Evangelical are responsible for 14% of the infant baptisms and14% of baptisms conducted among two to five year olds. On the other hand, the 16% of churches identified as Evangelical are responsible for 23% of baptisms conducted among fourteen to seventeen year olds and 17% of baptisms conducted among eighteen to twenty-one year olds.

Table 2 Baptisms

Age group	Total N	Evangelical N	Evangelical %	% churches Total	% churches Evangelical
under 2	195,990	27,320	14	74	75
2 – 5	10,640	1,510	14	21	22
6 – 9	3,650	550	15	12	12
10 – 13	3,170	470	15	11	11
14 – 17	1,590	360	23	6	9
18 – 21	1,010	170	17	4	4

The statistics indicate that although Evangelical churches may prefer to baptise individuals later in life they still baptise over 27,000 infants in a year. Taken seriously, this involves considerable investment in baptism preparation and considerable commitment to ongoing nurture among those baptised as infants. The Evangelical societies need to remain committed to the production of high-quality materials for use in preparation of those who present infants for baptism and to the training of clergy and laity for work in this area.

At the same time the statistics draw attention to the number of six to seventeen year olds being baptised in Evangelical churches and suggest the need for developing baptismal liturgy appropriately suited to the needs of these age groups. It is likely that many of those baptised as teenagers are also presented for confirmation.

Confirmation

The confirmation figures collected by the survey were also for the year 1985. Table 3 makes it clear that Evangelical churches are considerably more actively involved in presenting teenagers over the age of thirteen for confirmation than is the case throughout the Church of England as a whole. Overall the 16% of churches identified as Evangelical are responsible for 26% of all those confirmed between the ages of fourteen and twenty-one. This trend is complemented by a significant reluctance to confirm younger children. Thus the 16% of churches identified as Evangelical are responsible for just 8% of all those confirmed before their fourteenth birthday. When these two trends are balanced out, it emerges that the 16% of churches identified as Evangelical are responsible for 15% of the total number of confirmations conducted among those under the age of twenty-two.

These statistics indicate that Evangelical churches present nearly 5,000 candidates between the ages of fourteen and twenty-one for confirmation in a year. Taken seriously, this also involves considerable investment in confirmation preparation and considerable commitment to ongoing nurture within the Christian community. Again, the Evangelical societies need to remain committed to the production of high-quality materials suitable for confirmation preparation among these age groups and to the training of clergy and laity for work in this area.

Table 3 Confirmations

Age group	Total N	Evangelical N	Evangelical %	% churches Total	% churches Evangelical
6 – 9	380	60	16	1	1
10 – 13	28,860	2,380	8	33	22
14 – 17	15,940	4,010	25	37	36
18 – 21	2,850	890	31	8	14

Pre-School Provision

Parents and Toddlers

One way in which the Church of England is increasingly demonstrating its commitment to the very young and to their parents is through parent and toddler groups. Nationally about one church in six is offering this kind of facility, and making contact with over 76,600 children under the age of six, or about 2.1% of that age group. Table 4 suggests that the 16% of churches identified as Evangelical are responsible for 28% of this provision, well above the national average. The statistics indicate that Evangelical churches have contact with around 21,600 pre-schoolers and their parents through this facility.

Table 4 Parents and Toddlers

Age group	Total N	Evangelical N	Evangelical %	% churches Total	% churches Evangelical
under 2	35,600	10,450	29	15	24
2 – 5	41,010	11,150	27	15	23

Playgroups

Playgroups operate for slightly older children than parent and toddler groups and require more professional organisation. While nationally one church in six offers parent and toddler facilities, around one in fifteen offers some form of playgroup. These groups make contact with around 33,330 children under the age of six or a little under 1% of that age group. The playgroups operate mainly for two to five year olds, although it appears that a few younger babies also attend alongside their older brothers and sisters. Table 5 suggests that the 16% of churches identified as Evangelical are responsible for 28% of this provision, again well above the national average. The statistics indicate that Evangelical parishes have contact with over 9,300 pre-schoolers through this facility.

Table 5 Playgroups

Age group	Total N	Evangelical N	Evangelical %	% churches Total	% churches Evangelical
under 2	2,560	490	19	1	1
2 – 5	30,770	8,850	29	6	10

Taken together the statistics regarding parent and toddler groups and playgroups highlight the commitment of Evangelical parishes to working among pre-schoolers and their parents. The considerable investment in these areas needs to be matched by commitment to professional leadership training and the development of high quality curriculum materials.

Sunday School and CPAS Provisions

Sunday Schools

The Sunday school has become a generic name for the Church's work among children. It is not unusual to hear the Friday afternoon activity club referred to as a Sunday school, although it neither resembles school nor takes place on Sunday.

Nationally the main age group attracted by Sunday schools is the six to nine year olds. Currently Sunday schools make contact with over 129,000 six to nine year olds, or about 6% of that age group. Many Sunday schools begin recruiting significantly before the age of beginning day school. Currently Sunday schools make contact with nearly 72,000 two to five year olds, or about 3% of that age group. Some Sunday schools even welcome babies under the age of two years. Sunday schools tend to lose their members after the age of nine, but nationally there are still around 60,000 ten to thirteen year olds in contact with Sunday school or about 2.5% of that age group.

It is likely that many of the fourteen to seventeen year olds and eighteen to twenty-one year olds in contact with Sunday schools are functioning as teachers or helpers.

Table 6 suggests that the 16% of churches identified as Evangelical are responsible for nearly 18% of the young people who come into contact with Anglican Sunday schools. This table also draws attention to the comparatively high proportion of babies involved in Sunday school provision among Evangelical churches. The 16% of churches identified as Evangelical are responsible for 33% of the under two year olds who attend Sunday school. These very young children will require special attention and provision if work with them is to be safe and effective.

Table 6 Sunday Schools

Age group	Total N	Evangelical N	Evangelical %	% churches Total	% churches Evangelical
under 2	5,040	1,650	33	7	11
2 – 5	71,620	13,180	18	46	43
6 – 9	129,410	21,770	17	51	47
10 – 13	60,070	10,920	18	42	39
14 – 17	11,850	2,230	19	19	17
18 – 21	2,950	630	21	9	10

The statistics also show that the recruitment and lapsation pattern among Evangelical churches follows a similar pattern to that experienced throughout the Church of England. Further interpretation of these statistics needs to wait, however, until another description of work among children and young people has also been taken into account.

CPAS Organisations

The Church Pastoral Aid Society organisations contribute a national framework for nurturing activities among children and young people through Scramblers, Climbers, Pathfinders, Explorers and the Church Youth Fellowship Association. Churches which participate in these schemes tend to operate them as their main form of work among children and young people. Throughout the Church of England as a whole about one church in nine claims to be operating CPAS related schemes. These schemes begin to recruit members during the pre-school years and continue to increase membership into the early teens, making their greatest impact among ten to thirteen year olds. Among this age group they contact over 28,000 individuals, or 1.2% of the population.

Table 7 suggests that the 16% of the churches identified as Evangelical are responsible for 65% of the young people who come into contact with CPAS organisations. This high percentage accurately reflects the fact that the CPAS is firmly located within the Evangelical wing of the church.

Table 7 CPAS Organisations

Age group	Total N	Evangelical N	Evangelical %	% churches Total	% churches Evangelical
under 2	1,150	880	77	1	4
2 – 5	11,730	8,340	71	5	19
6 – 9	21,570	14,260	66	6	23
10 – 13	28,360	17,560	62	10	34
14 – 17	15,680	10,320	66	7	29
18 – 21	3,620	2,360	65	4	15

Summary

A fair appreciation of the comparable strength of Evangelical churches' work among children and young people can only be achieved by aggregating the information presented for Sunday schools and CPAS organisations. From table 8 it can be seen that overall the Church of England has contact with around 83,300 two to five year olds, or about 3.5% of that age group, around 51,000 six to nine year olds, or about 6.7% of that age group, around 88,400 ten to thirteen year olds, or about 3.8% of that age group, and 27,500 fourteen to seventeen year olds, or about 1% of that age group.

Table 8 Summary: Sunday Schools and CPAS

Age group	Total N	Evangelical N	Evangelical %	% churches Total	% churches Evangelical
under 2	6,190	2,530	41	8	15
2 – 5	83,350	21,530	26	50	61
6 – 9	150,980	36,030	24	56	67
10 – 13	88,430	28,480	32	48	63
14 – 17	27,520	12,560	46	26	42
18 – 21	6,560	2,990	46	12	23

These statistics suggest that the 16% of churches identified as Evangelical are responsible for about 27% of the young people under the age of fourteen who come into contact with Sunday schools or similar forms of activity. At the same time, the very presence of over 88,500 under fourteen year olds participating in Sunday school type provision in Evangelical churches highlights the commitment of the Evangelical movement to ministry among children and emphasises the importance of the considerable investment made by Evangelical societies in Sunday school curriculum and leadership training.

Service Participation

Church Choirs

If children now leave Sunday school around the age of nine within the Church of England as a whole it is often the choir which provides their next firm link with the church. Church choirs nationally make contact with nearly 31,000 ten to thirteen year olds, or about 1.3% of that age group. Many choirs start recruiting children considerably under the age of ten. Nationally there are around 12,400 six to nine year olds in church choirs, or about 0.5% of that age group. After the age of thirteen there is a sharp decline in the number of choristers.

Table 9 makes it clear that although Evangelical churches have contact with many more young people through Sunday school type activities, they have contact with a smaller number of young people through church choirs. Thus the 16% of churches identified as Evangelical make contact with just 11% of the children and young people between the ages of six and twenty-one who are involved in church choirs. While in the Church of England as a whole one in three churches has contact with ten to thirteen year olds through participation in church choirs, among Evangelical churches the proportion falls to one in four.

Table 9 Church Choir

Age group	Total N	Evangelical N	Evangelical %	% churches Total	% churches Evangelical
6 – 9	12,400	1,400	11	21	15
10 – 13	30,860	3,100	10	34	24
14 – 17	15,250	1,830	12	28	23
18 – 21	4,940	740	15	14	13

These findings may reflect the preference of some Evangelical churches to promote their ministry among children and young people largely through specialist children and youth ministries rather than through participation in the liturgy. At the same time the statistics indicate that over 7,000 children and young people are currently participating in church choirs in Evangelical churches. Evangelical churches need to be well equipped and resourced to make good use of the potential provided through such contact.

Most of the churches which invite children and young people to join the choir also make arrangements for some kind of choir practice. The national data demonstrate that 88% of the ten to thirteen year old, 86% of the fourteen to seventeen year old and 82% of the eighteen to twenty-one year old choristers are also involved in a regular practice, which provides them with another significant point of contact with the church and may involve some form of instruction. On the other hand, some church choirs do not offer this additional point of contact for their children and young people.

Comparison of the figures presented in tables 9 and 10 suggest that Evangelical churches which have young people in their choir may be slightly less likely to provide choir practice opportunities for them. While nationally 87% of the children and young people involved in church choirs are also involved in choir practices, the proportion falls marginally in Evangelical churches to 85%.

Table 10 Choir Practice

Age group	Total N	Evangelical N	Evangelical %	% churches Total	Evangelical
6 – 9	11,150	1,220	11	19	13
10 – 13	27,100	2,690	10	30	20
14 – 17	13,050	1,500	11	24	18
18 – 21	4,050	590	15	11	10

Servers

Like singing in the church choir, serving at the altar provides another traditional point of contact between children and young people and the church. While church choirs, however, are clearly losing their members after the age of thirteen, within the Church of England as a whole serving continues to recruit young people in the fourteen to seventeen age group.

Table 11 clearly confirms the view that Evangelical churches are much less likely to recruit young people as servers and that, when they do so, they tend to recruit servers from an older age. Overall the 16% of churches identified as Evangelical are responsible for less than 3% of the children and young people involved as servers. At the same time, these statistics indicate that a small number of Evangelical churches are exploring how children and young people can be involved in the liturgy in this way.

Table 11 Servers

Age group	Total N	Evangelical N	Evangelical %	% churches Total	% churches Evangelical
6 – 9	1,520	10	1	4	0
10 – 13	10,230	120	1	19	2
14 – 17	15,070	500	3	26	6
18 – 21	5,350	200	4	14	4

Bell Ringers

Many churches which possess a ring of bells make a point of recruiting young people. The national data demonstrate that nearly a third (31%) of the churches which have a group of ringers involve under fourteen year old boys in this activity, while a quarter (26%) involve girls of this age group. The majority of churches which have young ringers appear to recruit only one or two.

Table 12 Bell Ringers

Age group	Total N	Evangelical N	Evangelical %	% churches Total	% churches Evangelical
6 – 9	370	40	11	1	0
10 – 13	4,030	530	13	9	7
14 – 17	6,720	850	13	14	11
18 – 21	4,090	470	11	10	7

Table twelve indicates that the 16% of churches identified as Evangelical make contact with 12% of the six to twenty-one year olds involved in church bell ringing. Not only are Evangelical churches generally less inclined to involve young people in this kind of activity, they also emerge as less able or willing than other churches to retain the involvement of their eighteen to twenty-one year old ringers. Overall these statistics suggest that Evangelical churches have contact with around 1,900 children and young people through bell ringing.

Uniformed Groups

Scouts and Guides

Brownies, Guides, Cubs and Scouts provide a very significant point of contact between a number of parish churches and young people. Historically many groups were sponsored by churches, and others have become identified with a church because they meet in a church hall or because churchgoers play a key role in their leadership. Nationally nearly one in five (18%) of the churches feel that they have a regular relationship with some aspect of the scouting movement among boys or girls.

These organisations are particularly important in helping the churches to have contact with six to nine year olds. Moreover, although the active membership decreases after the age of nine, there is still a large number of ten to thirteen year olds involved in church-related groups.

Table 13 Church Sponsored Scouts and Guides

Age group	Total N	Evangelical N	Evangelical %	% churches Total	% churches Evangelical
2 – 5	350	130	37	0	0
6 – 9	98,500	15,740	16	17	18
10 – 13	81,930	13,000	16	17	18
14 – 17	25,190	3,700	15	13	14
18 – 21	5,390	640	12	7	7

Table 13 indicates that Evangelical churches are neither more nor less successful than other churches in having contact with children and young people through church-sponsored Scouts and Guides. Thus overall the 16% of churches identified as Evangelical are responsible for 16% of the young people involved in church-sponsored Scouts, Guides, Cubs and Brownies. These statistics suggest that Evangelical churches currently have contact with over 28,000 children and young people between the ages of six and thirteen through church-sponsored Scouts, Guides, Cubs and Brownies, and that nearly one Evangelical church in every five is involved in these activities. The Evangelical societies, therefore, should not underestimate the importance of helping Evangelical parishes to make best use of the potential afforded through contacts with church-related Scout and Guide groups.

In addition to these church-related groups, a number of Brownie, Guide, Cub and Scout groups which are not church-related provide opportunities for church contact for children and young people through attendance at such events as parade services. If these groups are taken into account in addition to those described above, the number of children and young people who are in touch with the churches through scouting organisations is increased considerably.

The national data demonstrate that Cubs and Scouts bring Church of England churches into contact from time to time with about 5.9% of the nation's six to nine year old boys, about 4.9% of the nation's ten to thirteen year old boys and about 1.5% of the nation's fourteen to seventeen year old boys. Similarly Brownies and Guides bring Church of England churches into contact from time to time with about 9.1% of the nation's six to nine year old girls, about 7.2% of the nation's ten to thirteen year old girls and about 1.5% of the nation's fourteen to seventeen year old girls.

Table 14 indicates that Evangelical churches have a slight edge over other churches when non-church sponsored Scout and Guide groups are also brought into the picture. Thus overall the 16% of churches identified as Evangelical are responsible for 17% of the young people brought into contact with the church through Scouts, Guides, Cubs and Brownies. These statistics suggest that Evangelical churches currently have contact with over 52,000 children and young people between the ages of six and thirteen through the wider sphere of Scouts, Guides, Cubs and Brownies, and that one Evangelical church in every three is involved in this way. The Evangelical societies, therefore, should not underestimate the importance of helping Evangelical parishes to make best use of the potential afforded through such occasions as parade services, St George's Day and Thinking Day.

Table 14 Total Scout and Guide Contact

Age group	Total N	Evangelical N	Evangelical %	% churches Total	% churches Evangelical
2 – 5	720	180	25	0	0
6 – 9	167,760	28,910	17	29	32
10 – 13	141,730	23,820	17	29	32
14 – 17	42,860	6,400	15	21	24
18 – 21	9,000	1,290	14	11	10

Church Uniformed Groups

Historically the Boys' Brigade and the Girls' Brigade on the one hand and the Church Lads' and Church Girls' Brigade on the other hand have their roots in different church traditions. Tables 15 and 16 confirm that these historic differences remain highly significant for present practice, but that there is also considerable flexibility in the types of churches which relate to these groups.

Table 15 Boys' Brigade and Girls' Brigade

Age group	Total N	Evangelical N	Evangelical %	% churches Total	% churches Evangelical
2 – 5	350	130	37	0	1
6 – 9	4,540	1,400	31	1	3
10 – 13	4,130	1,470	36	1	3
14 – 17	2,130	770	36	1	3
18 – 21	370	140	38	1	2

The national data demonstrate that a branch of the Boys' Brigade or Girls' Brigade which caters for under fourteen year olds is present in about one Anglican church in sixty-five. Overall the 16% of churches identified as Evangelical are responsible for 34% of the children and young people contacted through the Boys' Brigade or Girls' Brigade.

Table 16 Church Lads' and Church Girls' Brigade

Age group	Total N	Evangelical N	Evangelical %	% churches Total	% churches Evangelical
6 – 9	2,670	380	14	1	1
10 – 13	3,010	390	13	1	1
14 – 17	2,000	300	15	1	1
18 – 21	530	80	15	1	0

The national data demonstrate that a branch of the Church Lads' and Church Girls' Brigade is present in about one Anglican church in eighty. Overall the 16% of churches identified as Evangelical are responsible for 14% of the children and young people contacted through the Church Lads' and Church Girls' Brigade.

While the Boys' Brigade, the Girls' Brigade and the Church Lads' and Church Girls' Brigade all have their major emphasis among six to thirteen year olds, they retain a much higher proportion of their membership into the fourteen to seventeen age group than the scouting organisations. Taken together the statistics indicate that these uniformed groups currently enable Evangelical churches to have contact with about 1,780 six to nine year olds, about 1,860 ten to thirteen year olds and about 1,070 fourteen to seventeen year olds. This is not an inconsiderable influence.

Other Uniformed Groups

In addition to the church-related uniformed groups, the Brownie, Guide, Cub and Scout groups, there is a range of other uniformed groups which bring children and young people into contact with the churches through such occasions as parade services.

Table 17 Other Uniformed Groups

Age group	Total N	Evangelical N	Evangelical %	% churches Total	% churches Evangelical
2 – 5	230	80	35	0	0
6 – 9	3,880	1,420	37	1	2
10 – 13	4,070	1,040	26	1	2
14 – 17	3,330	590	18	1	1
18 – 21	580	30	5	1	0

Table 17 demonstrates that the 16% of churches identified as Evangelical are responsible for 26% of the children and young people contacted through these other uniformed groups. The statistics indicate that Evangelical churches have contact with around 3,160 children and young people between the ages of six and twenty-one through these groups.

Youth Provision

Youth Clubs

Like 'Sunday school', 'youth club' is a generic term which covers a range of church provision for young people. While Sunday schools major particularly on six to nine year olds, youth clubs concentrate on ten to seventeen year olds. Nationally youth clubs make contact with around 44,350 ten to thirteen year olds, or about 1.9% of that age group, and with almost 48,000 fourteen to seventeen year olds, or about 1.7% of that age group.

Table 18 suggests that the 16% of churches identified as Evangelical are responsible for 20% of the young people who come into contact with Anglican youth clubs. While throughout the Church of England as a whole 20% of churches run some form of youth club for fourteen to seventeen year olds, the proportion rises to 24% among Evangelical churches. These figures demonstrate a higher commitment to youth work among Evangelical parishes.

Table 18 Youth Clubs

Age group	Total N	Evangelical N	Evangelical %	% churches Total	% churches Evangelical
6 – 9	9,300	1,890	20	5	5
10 – 13	44,350	7,130	16	19	17
14 – 17	47,930	10,620	22	20	24
18 – 21	8,890	2,510	28	9	12

116 470 22150 = 20%

The statistics suggest that Evangelical churches currently have contact with around 17,750 young people between the ages of ten and seventeen through youth club provisions. Again, these findings emphasise the importance of Evangelical societies adequately servicing such a large constituency of young people active within the parishes.

Girls' Friendly Society

The national data demonstrate that a branch of the Girls' Friendly Society which caters for under fourteen year olds is present in about one Anglican church in every 130.

Table 19 Girls' Friendly Society

Age group	Total N	Evangelical N	Evangelical %	% churches Total	% churches Evangelical
6 – 9	1,190	160	13	1	0
10 – 13	1,060	60	6	1	0
14 – 17	370	10	3	1	0
18 – 21	60	0	0	0	0

Table 19 demonstrates that the Girls' Friendly Society is not well represented in Evangelical churches. Thus, the 16% of churches identified as Evangelical are responsible for less than 9% of the girls contacted through this organisation. All told in the Evangelical churches this amounts to fewer than 250 girls and young women.

The Sunday Picture

In the preceding sections we have reviewed the numbers of children and young people who come into contact with the churches through specific provisions, like Sunday schools, church choirs and the various uniformed groups, in order to profile the comparative contribution of Evangelical churches. This final section asks a different kind of question by focusing attention on the total number of children and young people who come into contact with Anglican churches on a typical Sunday. These two approaches provide complementary information.

The total number of children and young people listed under Sunday schools, for example, may be considerably greater than the number who attend Sunday school on any given Sunday. Most Sunday schools cannot expect the whole of their roll to come on every occasion and some Sunday schools meet less frequently than every week. Similarly, the uniformed organisations may attend Sunday church services for a monthly parade service, or less frequently. On the other hand, in addition to the provisions made by the churches specifically for children and young people a number of children and young people come into regular contact with the church through attending all-age services on a Sunday.

Another section of the questionnaire, therefore, asked churches to make a careful list of all their Sunday services and activities, including creches, Sunday schools, 'junior church', youth groups and so on. When all this information is aggregated, the data show the total number of children and young people who have contact with the churches on a typical Sunday.

All told, on a typical Sunday the Church of England has contact nationally with over 22,000 under two year olds, or 1.8% of that age group; nearly 73,000 two to five year olds, or 3.1% of that age group; over 152,000 six to nine year olds, or 6.8% of that age group; nearly 138,000 ten to thirteen year olds, or 5.9% of that age group; over 93,000 fourteen to seventeen year olds, or 3.2% of that age group; and nearly 52,000 eighteen to twenty-one year olds, or 1.7% of that age group.

Table 20 Sunday Attendance

Age group	Total N	Evangelical N	Evangelical %	% churches Total	% churches Evangelical
under 2	22,370	6,230	28	37	49
2 – 5	72,680	18,020	25	57	67
6 – 9	152,130	31,590	21	65	73
10 – 13	137,850	28,030	20	65	73
14 – 17	93,350	23,030	25	57	65
18 – 21	51,570	16,940	33	43	53

From table twenty it is clear that Evangelical churches perform well above the national average. Thus, the 16% of churches identified as Evangelical are responsible for 23% of the total number of young people under the age of twenty-two who come into contact with the Church of England on a typical Sunday. While throughout the Church of England as a whole 65% of churches have contact with at least one six to nine year old on a typical Sunday, the proportion rises to 73% among Evangelical churches.

The statistics indicate that on a typical Sunday Evangelical churches have contact with nearly 124,000 young people under the age of twenty-two. Such a major cohort of young people deserves the best that the Evangelical societies can offer.

Conclusion

The figures presented in this study clearly indicate the continuing commitment of Evangelical churches to work among children and young people. This commitment is expressed especially strongly through the provision of special groups and activities where the emphasis can be on teaching and nurture in the faith. Such work needs to be supported by good-quality syllabuses and curriculum materials which successfully link the key elements of the faith with the young person's experiences of learning and life at school and at home.

Following the emphases of the British Council of Churches' report, *The Child in the Church*, published in 1976[21], and the Church of England's report, *Children in the Way*, published in 1988[22], it is important that clear links are made between the experiences of Sunday school-type provisions and the experiences of the adult church.

This study highlights the particular commitment of Evangelical churches to work among the very young and among their parents. In view of this, there must be a special concern among adult congregations to ensure that work with such groups commands the resources and the environment necessary to operate safely and effectively.

While there is much in this study to affirm the success of Evangelical churches in work among children and young people, there is no room for complacency. The report from the General Synod Board of Education and Board of Mission, *All God's Children*[23], draws upon the national statistics presented in this study to draw attention to the vast numbers of children and young people growing up outside the churches altogether.

All God's Children challenges the whole church to accept responsibility for evangelism among the young. The new information provided in the present study emphasises the special capability of Evangelical churches to respond to this challenge and to provide an example to the Church of England as a whole for the Decade of Evangelism.

Acknowledgements

The survey on which this paper is based was made possible by grants from the Central Board of Finance of the Church of England, The St Christopher's Trust, The All Saints' Educational Trust, The Hockerill Educational Foundation, The Foundation of St Mathias, St Gabriel's Trust, The Sarum St Michael Educational Charity and the Culham Trustees.

Notes

1. British Council of Churches, *The Child in the Church,* London, British Council of Churches, 1976.
2. Leslie J Francis, *Rural Anglicanism: a future for young Christians?*, London, Collins Liturgical Publications, 1985.
3. Board of Education, *Children in the Way: new directions for the Church's children,* London, National Society/Church House Publishing, 1988.
4. Leslie J Francis and David W Lankshear, *Continuing in the Way: Children, Young People and the Church,* London, National Society, 1991.
5. Leslie J Francis and David W Lankshear, The impact of church schools on village church life, *Educational Studies,* 16, 117-129, 1990.
6. Leslie J Francis and David W Lankshear, The impact of church schools on urban church life, *School Effectiveness and School Improvement,* 2, 324-335, 1991.
7. Leslie J Francis and David W Lankshear, The impact of children's work on village church life, *Spectrum,* 21, 35-45, 1992.
8. Leslie J Francis and David W Lankshear, Shared Pilgrimage: the impact of children's work on adult church membership, *Journal of Empirical Theology,* 4, 24-31, 1991.
9. David W Lankshear and Leslie J Francis, Pre-school provision in the rural church, *A Better Country,* 24, 28-29, 1991.
10. Leslie J Francis and David W Lankshear, Church provision for pre-school children: impact on urban church life, *Research in Education,* 48, 55-64, 1992.
11. David W Lankshear and Leslie J Francis, The use of the Revised Catechism in Anglican churches, *British Journal of Religious Education,* 13, 95-100, 1991.
12. Leslie J Francis and David W Lankshear, The rural rectory: the impact of a resident priest on local church life, *Journal of Rural Studies,* 8, 97-103, 1992.

13. Leslie J Francis and David W Lankshear, The impact of children's work on church life in hamlets and small villages, *Journal of Christian Education,* 35, 57-63, 1992.

14. Leslie J Francis and David W Lankshear, Do small churches hold a future for children and young people? *Modern Churchman,* 33, 15-19, 1991.

15. Leslie J Francis and David W Lankshear, Ageing Anglican clergy and performance indicators in the rural church, compared with the suburban church, *Ageing and Society,* 13, 339-363, 1993.

16. Leslie J Francis and David W Lankshear, Faith in the Isle of Wight: a profile of rural Anglicanism, *Contact,* 105, 28-33, 1991.

17. David W Lankshear, Marjorie Carnelley and Leslie J Francis, Special services and events, in *All God's Children,* pp 101-105, London, National Society/Church House Publishing, 1991.

18. see note 4 above.

19. L.J. Francis and D.W. Lankshear, *In the Catholic Way: Children, Young People and the Church in Catholic parishes of the Church of England,* London, National Society, 1995.

20. *The 1986 Population Estimates for England and Wales,* London, Office of Population Censuses and Surveys, 1987 (reference PPI 87/1 and Crown Copyright).

21. see note 1 above.

22. see note 3 above.

23. General Synod Board of Education and Board of Mission, *All God's Children? children's evangelism in crisis,* London, National Society/Church House Publishing, 1991.

The National Society

The National Society (Church of England) for Promoting Religious Education supports everyone involved in Christian education – teachers, school governors, students, parents, clergy, parish and diocesan education teams – with the resources of its RE centres, courses, conferences and archives.

Founded in 1811, the Society was cheifly responsible for setting up the nationwide network of Church shools in England and Wales, and still helps them with legal and administrative advice for head-teachers and governors. It was also a pioneer in teacher education through the Church colleges. The Society now provides resources for those responsible for RE and worship in any school, lectures and students in colleges, and clergy and lay people in parish education. It publishes a wide range of books and booklets and two magazines, *Crosscurrent* (free to members) and *Together with Children*.

The National Society is a voluntary body which works in partnership with the Church of England General Synod Board of Education and the Division for Education of the Church in Wales. An Anglican society, it also operates ecumenically, and helps to promote inter-faith education and dialogue through its RE centres.

For a resources catalogue and details of individual, corporate and associate membership contact:

The Promotions Officer
The National Society
Church House
Great Smith Street
London
SW1P 3NZ
Telephone: 0171-222 1672
Fax: 0171-233 2592